S.P.I.C.E.

Kimberly Mihaychuk

Print information available on the last page

Rev. date: 06/05/2019

To order additional copies of this book, contact:
Xlibris
1-888-795-4274
www.Xlibris.com
Orders@Xlibris.com

iNtRoductioN

I am Kimberly. A mother of two boys. I work as a Child Development Worker and have a Masters in TEFL teaching ESL.

I was 19 years old when I had my first son. I was very inexperienced, young, and single. I applied to college to major in architecture, moved my son and I, and chose a new life for us. As I attended college, obviously a part time job and daycare were needed. The owner of the daycare center offered me to work as the nursery teacher, and there began the start of my child education career. I attended another college doing part time and received my certificate in ELCC.

Fast forward 12 years later, my second son was born with the help of IVF. I went back to work at the center my son was attending daycare. After a year, I decided to stay at home and work part time. I do want my toddler to experience a similar environment as he did while at daycare. So, I came up with inexpensive brain building activities and games to promote, encourage, and develop his skills.

S.P.I.C.E. is a useful tool in aiding child development. It stands for Social, Physical, Intellectual, Creative, and Emotional. These skills can be learned through play.

This book is created for children from 18months-3years. It is intended to help the growth of their social, physical, intellectual, creative, and emotional development.

It consists of activities and games that are very inexpensive and uses many household items. Most items can be found at the local dollar store. Its also designed to be easy and child directed to promote cognitive skills, fine motor skills, gross motor skills, and problem solving.

This book is to help aid parents who work full time, who are new parents, parents with low income, single parents, busy parents, parents looking for bonding time, or parents looking for a few minutes to sip coffee.

Remember it is never about the finished product, but the process that is important.

CONTENTS

Social

Snowmen

You will Need: Snow, Sticks, Carrot, Scarf, Hat, Rocks
Skills Emphasized: Gross Motor, Fine Motor, Creative, Emotional

Do you want to build a Snowman? It is great to get outdoors, working together and getting exercise, Rolling the ball is the toughest part. Learning to gather a pile of snow and squish into a hard-round ball can take practice. Start one for the littles, so they can begin rolling it around, collecting the snow and making tracks.

Once it gets big e`nough, it is easier to push around. Until its too big, then its time to make the second one. This is a social activity. The littles need help to lift the snowballs on top of another, but they can pack extra snow to hold them in place for a sturdy snowman. Once there are two snowballs, the third one is much smaller.

Talk about what the snowman needs. The snowman needs arms, he needs two sticks for arms. Find two sticks. If you have extra hats or mitts, let the littles pick them out. Talk about how the snowman has a carrot nose and pick a carrot.

And whatever materials you have on hand to create is great to use. It is creative and encourages imagination. The things needed for this project listed above are just ideas, as anything can be used.

Snow Castles

You will need: Shovel, Bucket, Snow
Skills Emphasized: Gross Motor, Fine Motor, Social, Creative

Whether you live in warm weather with sand or cold weather with snow, a bucket and shovel can go a long way. Sand castles or Snow castles can be a great social tool as well as gross

motor exercise. BURN THE ENERGY. Learning to scoop and fill the bucket is a great developmental milestone. It helps with fine motor, and hand/eye coordination. The littles will need help packing the snow tight and help to flip it, creating the start of the sand castle. If you have beach toys, it works just as good in snow.

Also add on to the activity by adding food coloring and color the castle. And with imagination, a game of knights and dragons, or GI Joes can play using the snow castle. There are times when the snow is not sticky, but it becomes a great visual on the different snow types. Being little, the best part is stomping and kicking the snow castle over.

This can also be an open-ended activity. Make a big fort, or small castle. Add details to the castle and a moat. Use Lego as part of the structure. When the littles have an interest in something like a superhero, you can integrate the snow castles into any game or activity. Other ideas for the littles are to use it as a doll house, or use little people toys if any, and create a tower and play King Kong. Filling and dumping the bucket is a great activity too if the littles are wanting a simpler activity.

Shooting Snow with Colors

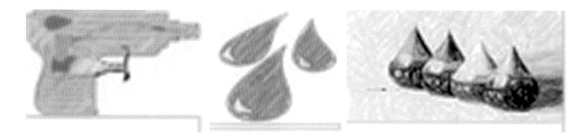

You will need: Small Water Gun, Water, Food Coloring
Skills Emphasized: Fine Motor, Gross Motor, Hand/Eye Coordination

Color the snow different colors with a water gun and create open ended activities outdoors. Mix the water and food coloring first, then pour it into the water gun for the littles. Then the littles can 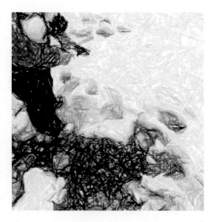 create drawings or squiggly lines in the snow. Try to create circles. Also make a target with a bull's eye out of snow and food coloring, you can even draw it out or a piece of paper can work too, and practice aiming and shooting the target. How about making a rainbow, and discuss the colors used, or ask what colors are used, color snowballs and count the colored ones versus the non-colored ones. Practice writing letters or writing numbers. Using letters and numbers can be extended for learning through play. Ask the littles to shoot at a certain color, number or letter. Color every third snowball. Learn the letters of their name in a way that is fun, interesting, and engaging. Create a trail to follow in the snow, or hopscotch. It would be fun jumping in the snow. And all this using a water gun. A spray bottle can work the same way using food coloring and water. With a spray bottle, the littles have the option on what kind of stream they would like to make. A mist, squirt, jet, or the shower setting. They can try them all, and see what each setting does, and talk about it.

Getting Dressed for Outside

You will need: Winter Gear
Skills Emphasized: Fine Motor, Language

Getting Dressed outside for winter is a lot of work. There are times the littles do not want to be dressed, or you get one dressed, and the other has stripped all the gear off. But there is a system. Whether you have one or more littles, getting them dressed in the same thing at the same time is much more efficient, and can get easier once they are able to help themselves.

Turning the transition in to a song. ♪ First, we put our pants on, our pants on, our pants on, first we put our pant on to go outside and play. Then we put our boots on, our boots on, our boots on. ♪ Normally boots would be last. It does make it more effiecient to put them on after snowpants. The more independent the littles get, the more the routing changes. Younger ones the gloves go on before the coat, so they are nicely tucked in. For the older littles, they may want to zip up their own coat. In this case the gloves are last. It is also eaiser for the littles to put on their own toques before the jacket as they have more mobility. Then you can adjust their toque before going outside.

physical

Sledding

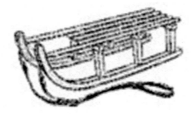

You will need: Sled

Skills Emphasized: Gross Motor, Social

Walking up those hills is great exercise for those littles that need to burn energy. As they get older, they can pull the sled

too. Riding together or allowing them to go themselves will always leave a smile on everyone's face. The best days are when it's a bit warmer and the snow is sticky. Small hills or big hills. Encourage the fear. Some littles are afraid with new or big things. And some littles are fearless.

It is a good idea to pull them around on a sled then try a small hill, try riding together. The littles will see your reaction, and decides how to feel about the experience, so make sure to have fun. Also remember, you are getting their energy out on the hill, not yours. So, if you are expecting to do all the work be prepared. Try to start with what the littles are comfortable with.

The older the littles are the more time they will spend on a specific activity. You can account for the littles enjoying an activity for five to ten minutes at the most before they move on to something else. They also tend to lose more energy with walking and hiking up hills, then a game of chase.

Of course, to finish off after sledding, add a cup of Hot Chocolate.

Rock Collecting in Snow

You will need: Bucket, Shovel
Skills Emphasized: Gross Motor, Creative

Those warm winter days when the snow is melting. Bring a bucket, and a shovel, and venture out around the block. During the walk, mention sight seeing and talk about what you see. Then find some small rocks, sticks leaves, whatever those little hearts desire. The littles may have to dig through the snow and fill a bucket. Then in a safe area where the melted snow is draining into the sewer, you can drop a rock one at a time into the grate. Let's listen to the sounds as the rocks fall, and the water streaming down. Count the rocks, count how long it takes for the rock to hit the water. Can you see the rock? Can you watch it fall? Does a big rock fit? How about a handful of rocks? Now try a chunk of snow. Does it have the same affect? Does the snow make sounds when it hits the water?

There is a lot of different things to learn create or experiment with nature. It is free. Creates a relaxing environment, and its natural. Its The fine details in life that stand out to the littles. They see and hear more than we can, there's minds are clear and absorb like a sponge.

Animal Footprints in Snow

<u>You will need:</u> Feet
Skills Emphasized: Gross Motor

Have you ever discovered different footprints animals make as they walk through the snow? We have many birds in our yard.

One snow day there were many rabbit tracks all over the yard too. In town we can spot deer tracks or puppy tracks. And With our feet, we can create tracks too. They can be more noticeable in snow, but this activity can be played anytime of year. Mud puddles work just as good as snow.

For the older littles, this can turn in to a small scavenger hunt with parent help. Find an animal print draw it on paper, doesn't have to be perfect. Make a print using a fist in paint or play dough. If you are aware of what kind of animal made the prints, talk about it. Or find the info and have a discussion later about the different shapes and sizes, some have two toes or hooves, others may have four.

Most all children want is to have you there with them and them be heard. The best is a nature walk through the forest. Or a nature center, bird sanctuary, and if you happen to camp, this is a great activity to play.

Sing with Paper Microphone

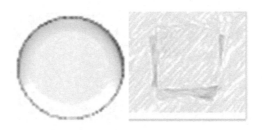

You will need: Paper, Ball
Skills Emphasized: Gross Motor, Creative, Emotional

Use a toy ball or something round and wrap paper around it and tape it. I find it easier and more stable with the ball. Or you can

scrunch paper into a ball shape. Then make a cone shape from another piece of paper and taped together to make a microphone. Singing helps vocabulary, language, sometimes pronunciation, and builds confidence. Music can always make a person feel amazing as it soothes the soul. Socialize with the littles and bring out the pots and pans to drum along.

This is a great activity for any age. If your little has an older sibling, the older sibling can get involved in imaginative play. Create a stage with blankets or boxes. Plan a rock band. Who plays what, come up with a name for the band and make decorations and create outfits. Drama play can be endless. All created with household items and other toys. A whole day of pretend play with many opportunities.

And think, all this from a simple, handmade paper microphone that was free to make. These activities can be used with any paper at home. Newspaper, magazines, flyers.

intellectual

Frozen Bubbles

<u>You will need:</u> 1/3cup Dawn Dish Soap, 1cup Water, 2Tbsp Corn-Starch, Bubble Wand, Plastic Container
Skills Emphasized: Fine Motor

Mix the ingredients together and place in fridge for an hour. On a cold day, blow the bubbles outside and watch them instantly freeze. Its beautiful and magical. It also helps the children practices blowing, exercising the lungs, coordination to blow from the bubble wand. Any body can enjoy bubbles, whether its chasing them, catching them or watching them pop. This also allows for cognitive development, and patience. For this to work best, a bubble needs to land on a surface without popping and encourage the littles to watch the bubble freeze. Knowing littles, they would want to catch and pop right away. Bubbles can make them over excited, so being able to catch their attention, communicate and observe is a huge milestone. Do it a few times yourself, once they inquire what is happening, they are more likely to try with caution.

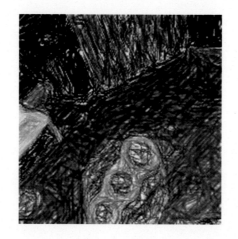

This can be considered as discovery and science activity. Adding social and creativity and fine motor.

Oobleck

<u>You will need:</u> Water, Corn-Starch, Plastic Container
Skills Emphasized: Fine Motor, Creative

Science is facinating at this age. I could just imagine what littles see through their eyes. Develpomenting cognitive skills, problem solving, and sensory skills. Add the water to corn starcth a bit at a time. And once you feel that it is the right consistency, let the play begin. This activity is like quicksand. Its hard at first to poke it. But then is like liquid when items are placed in it.

Add on other activities to this. Place treasure in the mix and have the littles search for it, trying to dig it out when its hard, or find a way to make it gooey. Play with animals or other toys in the mix. Or just fun with fingers. The littles can feel the gooey texture running through their fingers and try to mold it. Learning to write or trace letters in the mix is a great activity for the older littles.

Color can also be added to this as well for more enrichment. Make it brown and imagine a desert. Make it blue and imagine the ocean, make it green and imagine earthquakes and sink holes.

Chemical Reaction

You will need: Baking Soda, Vinegar, Food Coloring, Eye Dropper, Plastic Container
Skills Emphasized: Fine Motor, Creative

Mix the vinegar and food coloring together, and place baking soda in a separate container. Eye droppers work best, but we had a syringe, the food coloring allows the littles see the

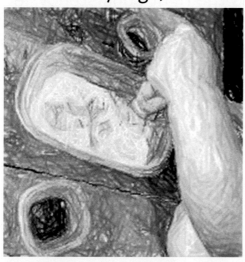

reaction, as it is more visible than just plain vinegar. Using just an eye dropper will allow more control and wont flow over, so it makes this a continuous play experiment.

It bubbles very well, and the littles can use the imagination and pretend it's a bubbly swamp or lava. Count how long it bubbles, talk about colors, even mix colors, red and blue will create purple bubbles.

There is a volcano project that can be done with older littles as they can build a volcano using a bottle, and glue on scrunches of paper, build a mountain and paint it too. And add the same ingredients just in a larger quantity. Also, if you fill the bottom of the bottle in the mountain with water, it will help make a larger explosion, especially if the older littles made a tall mountain. The volcano project is more of a one-time experiment and very messy, so be aware of where you place the volcano.

Snowflake Sensory Bottle

You will need: Water Bottle, Food Coloring, Styrofoam Bits, Glitter

Skills Emphasized: Fine Motor, Emotional

Mix the ingredients together and place in into a bottle and seal the lid. Sensory bottles can be used as a calm down mechanism when the littles are feeling anxious or overstimulated. Or during down time. It is a individual activity to help the littles recharge with positive energy.

They can be made into rain sticks using big straws cut into smallers pieces and rice. Then shake it and tip it upside down. You can hear the rice flow through the straws. Make musical instruments using small bells or other hard objects inside the bottle and shake away.

Also you can make one designed to go with a story for story time. Bedtime would be great time for a quiet story and a sensory bottle. The story for example,can be about a captain out in sea. Create blue liquid and place a boat inside the bottle. The littles can tip it back and forth and watch the boat float along the waves.

Other great ones are hide and seek bottles. Fill one with leaves and sticks and small toy bugs. Can you spot the ladybug? Or letters. Can you find the letters in your name

CREATIVE

Snow and Dump Trucks

You will need: Toy Truck, Snow, Plastic Container
Skills Emphasized: Fine Motor, Creative, Emotional

To cold to go outside for snow play? Lets grab a container, fill it with snow and bring the snow inside. We could also use some cars or trucks to play in the snow with. And let the imagaination soar. Maybe we are cleaning the roads on a snowy day. Create a hill for the cars to drive down and have a race. Add another container to practice scooping and dumping the snow from one container to another. Or a treasure hunt for letters, colored ice cubes, magnets.Whatever you have that you can bury into the snow. As we play with it, it will melt, the snow slowly dissapears, now are trucks are flooding, and the ice cubes or icebergs are melting and moving in the water. Time to get out the boats and fish. You can also stir in glitter or other ingredients.

Ask questions like, hot or cold, solid or liquid. Add science and chemistry into the mix and explain the differences.

The best part about this activity as a parent is two containers and snow. It was a proud moment of endless creativity. It did not cost a thing and the littles are developing hand and eye coordination, cognitive development, creativity and language, and fine motor skills.

Water painting

You will need: Water, Paint Brush, Plastic Container
Skills Emphasized: Fine Motor, Creative

Keeping the little busy at times while cooking or cleaning can

be hard. Give the littles non-messy paint, Water. And a paint brush. And let them paint the fridge, pantry door, whatever. Water is not going to hurt nothing, so the littles are able to be entertained without worry.

Use a container with a lid and small hole, so they can dip the paintbrush in without pouring the water out. I used a snack container that has a lid meant for the littles hand to go in, but nothing is poured out. They can paint the fridge, cupboards baseboards, dishwasher. The littles are in eye view and occupied.

As it dries the littles can do another lap around the kitchen. This is great as they are cleaning at the same time. They are more likely to paint over a spot they see.

This is great for developing fine motor skills. Talk about the things in the kitchen, make it a game, talk about the art they create. This allows you to bond and spend time together while doing chores.

Laundry Basket String Maze

You will need: Laundry Basket, String, Tongs, Small Objects
Skills Emphasized: Fine Motor, Intellectual, Emotional

Tie string back and forth through a laundry basket creating a spider web or weave idea. Place small objects, toys, balls at the bottom in the basket. And the littles can use the tongs or hands to maneuver through the string and try to pick up the objects.

This can be used a lot during parties or any indoor activities. Birthday party themed, Halloween themed, try to pick the spider up. Easter or any other holiday that includes games and groups of littles.

For the older littles they can use the thongs. It is good find motor hand eye coordination and problem solving. This activity is like a puzzle, and I believe puzzles feed the brain.

Puppet Play

You will need: Sock

Skills Emphasized: Fine Motor, Creative, Emotional, Social

Sock puppets. Luckily most littles have decorative socks. As they outgrow them, use them for sock puppets. They can be decorated or used as is.

As you chose, you can add googly eyes and yarn for hair, tongue.

Puppet play can be expressed through drama play, role play, creativity, socializing. It can create storytelling, action. This brings the littles out of their shell. Using a puppet to talk for them, and they believe it to be true. The littles can then express a variety of emotional, social creativity.

This can also help aide in the development of language, and emotional insight. Using puppets as parents to enjoy in the play or teaching them manners and emotions in a fun and healthy way.

EMotioNal

Emotional Faces

You will need: Popsicle Sticks, Paper
Skills Emphasized: Social, Intellectual, Emotional

Create simple emoji faces out of paper and tape them to the popsicle sticks. The littles are at a point where they are expressing emotions and we as adults must teach how to communicate those emotions in a positive manner. Happy, sad, tired, and angry are the main emotions we feel daily.

Make a game of it. Of course, introduce the different emotions by modelling. Make the face and add in a sentence, I feel sad, or I feel angry. The little will see your body language and understand what sad looks like and what angry looks like. Then the littles can copy the facial expressions.

Help them repeat the word that fits each expression. A part of expressing emotions is being able to say how you feel and allow them to feel comfortable to express that with you.

Then communicate how you feel in a positive way to teach management skills when feeling an emotion.

Play Babies

You will need: Baby Doll

Skills Emphasized: Gross Motor, Intellectual, Creative

Teaching the littles how to be caring. And gentle, taking care of something or someone. It is not just for girls. Boys are just as important as we want them to treat others with respect and be gentlemen.  The little mimic what they learn and see. They are caring out routines during play. Hand a little a doll, they will rock it, feed it, make it a bed. Possibly say no to the doll. This is also important to observe healthy behaviour.

Although some children may play alone, Socializing is a developmental skill when participating in dramatic play. Sharing, taking turns, making conversation, learning language, emotions, empathy, and create stories to play. For example, someone is the mommy, someone is the baby, and someone is the family pet.

Other role playing games may include cops and robbers, dinosaurs, super heroes, and Prince and Princess.

Flashlight Story Reading

You will need: Book, Flashlight, Blanket
Skills Emphasized: Fine Motor, Creative, Intellectual, Emotional

During the day or before bedtime, a blanket fort can be a great social activity. For some littles, it can be a place t be calm. A place that is quiet. It also can be an emotional place. That comfort your little will receive from you is most important to them and their development. If you pretend to hide under the blanket, maybe a family pet comes and finds you both. Or a story with a flashlight.

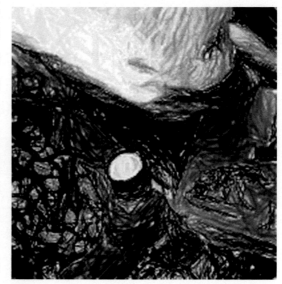

The forts can create a warm environment to start a nice quiet activity. Especially for the children who do not nap anymore. Down time is still essential in their every day health. It is based on each individual child, but the littles need power up activities as well as power down.

So, grab your favorite book and imagine in the fort you are apart of the story with your little. Once your little has had enough quiet time or down time. Make a fort out of the living room, create a cave for animal play or dungeons and dragons.

Whatever interest your little is in can create a whole day of play inside or outside.

Dress Up

You will need: Dress Up Clothes
Skills Emphasized: Goss Motor, Creative, Emotional

Have you ever watched Mr. Dress up and his tickle trunk? Everyone loves to dress up.

At this age it is important not to define gender specific toys for play. Allowing a little to express their creativity is what is

most important. They do not understand that play dresses are only for girls. That is something that adults teach them. Eventually there will be a time where they start to learn and understand there are girls and boys, at that point, things can be more gender specific but not limited to.

The play is endless with dress up. The littles can be any character they want to be. Dress up as superhero's, princess, magician, worker, baker, and many more. It doesn't even have to be a character. A tutu and top hat to dance in, or skip, hop and jump. The littles can wear different things while playing others thing like Lego or movie night.

This Book is Based On

Mama's Cheap Toddler Fun

for Busy Toddlers

https://www.facebook.com/Mamas-Cheap-Toddler-Fun-for-Busy-Toddlers-246271549405641/

By Kimberly

Printed in the United States
By Bookmasters